CELEBRATE THE UNITED STATES!

WHY DO WE HAVE A NATIONAL ANTHEM?

T0805957

BY BEATRICE HARRIS

Gareth Stevens PUBLISHING

Please visit our website, www.garethstevens.com. For a free color catalog of all our high-quality books, call toll free 1-800-542-2595 or fax 1-877-542-2596.

Library of Congress Cataloging-in-Publication Data
Names: Harris, Beatrice, author.
Title: Why do we have a national anthem? / Beatrice Harris.
Description: Buffalo, New York : Gareth Stevens Publishing, 2026. | Series: Celebrate the United States! | Includes index.
Identifiers: LCCN 2024061758 (print) | LCCN 2024061759 (ebook) | ISBN 9781482471151 (library binding) | ISBN 9781482471144 (paperback) | ISBN 9781482471168 (ebook)
Subjects: LCSH: Baltimore, Battle of, Baltimore, Md., 1814–Juvenile literature. | Star-spangled banner (Song)–Juvenile literature.
Classification: LCC E356.B2 H3 2026 (print) | LCC E356.B2 (ebook) | DDC 973.5/2–dc23/eng/20250213
LC record available at https://lccn.loc.gov/2024061758
LC ebook record available at https://lccn.loc.gov/2024061759

Published in 2026 by
Gareth Stevens Publishing
2544 Clinton Street
Buffalo, NY 14224

Copyright © 2026 Gareth Stevens Publishing

Designer: Jeffrey Taylor
Editor: Therese Shea

Photo credits: Series art (blue background) Paladin12/Shutterstock.com; Cover, p. 1 AI Generated/Shutterstock.com; p. 5 YES Market Media/Shutterstock.com; p. 7 Focus Pix/Shutterstock.com; p. 9 Everett Collection/Shutterstock.com; p. 11 Walters Art Museum/commons.wikimedia.org; p. 13 Dr.frog/commons.wikimedia.org; p. 14 (Inset) Frank A. O'Connell, Wilbur F. Coyle/commons.wikimedia.org; p. 15 Frank A. O'Connell, Wilbur F. Coyle/commons.wikimedia.org; p. 17 Thomas Carr/commons.wikimedia.org; p. 19 sirtravelalot/Shutterstock.com; p. 21 Limolida Design Studio/Shutterstock.com.

All rights reserved. No part of this book may be reproduced in any form without permission in writing from the publisher, except by a reviewer.

Printed in the United States of America

Some of the images in this book illustrate individuals who are models. The depictions do not imply actual situations or events.

CPSIA compliance information: Batch #CS26GS: For further information contact Gareth Stevens at 1-800-542-2595.

Find us on

CONTENTS

Boldface words appear in the glossary.

A Special Song

If you like sports, you've likely noticed an event at the beginning of many games. Everyone is asked to stand and someone sings a certain song. It's called the national anthem. An anthem is a song that **celebrates** a people or a country.

Our Anthem

Most countries around the world have a national anthem. The government chooses the song to **represent** the country. When people sing their country's anthem, they're showing patriotism, or support and love for their country. The U.S. national anthem is called "The Star-**Spangled** Banner."

Rio2016
TEDD
EN O
CLUB JUDO

Written in Battle

The words of "The Star-Spangled Banner" were written during the War of 1812. This war was fought between Great Britain and the United States between 1812 and 1815. In 1814, British soldiers set fire to buildings in Washington, D.C. They took some Americans as **prisoners**.

Doctor William Beanes was held prisoner on a British ship near Baltimore, Maryland. His friend, Francis Scott Key, sailed out to ask the British to **release** Beanes. They agreed, but the Americans weren't allowed to leave until the Battle of Baltimore was over. Key watched from the water as the British attacked the city of Baltimore on September 13, 1814.

Francis Scott Key

For hours, Key watched as British ships in Baltimore Harbor fired on Fort McHenry. The **bombardment** continued all day and throughout the night. He could see the British navy's firepower "bursting in air." In the morning, he saw the U.S. flag still flying over the fort.

Key was happy to see the American "star-spangled banner" still flying. It meant the United States had won. He began to write a **poem** he called "Defence of Fort M'Henry" on the back of a letter. He finished it when he and his friends finally got to shore.

the Fort McHenry flag

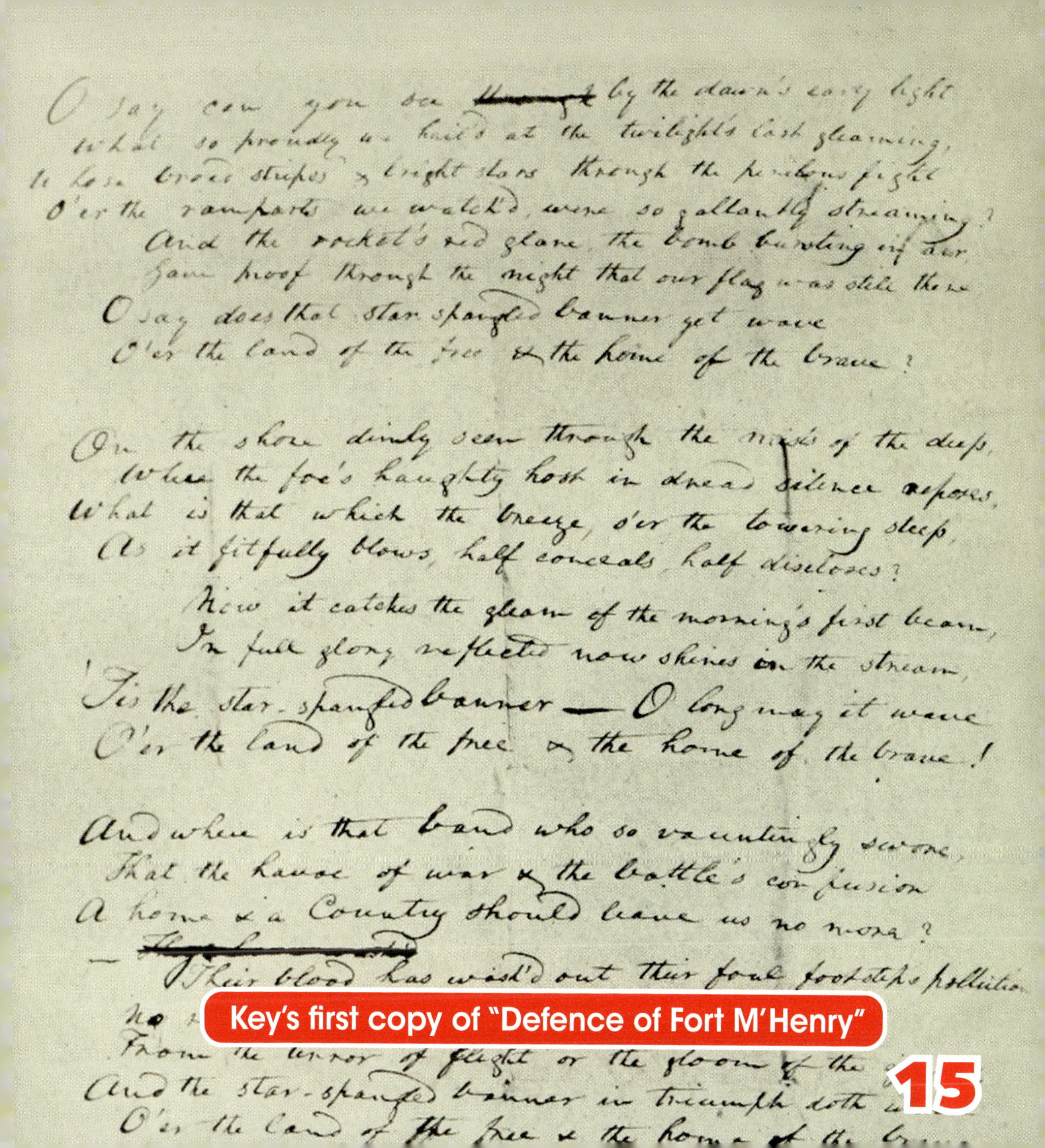
O say can you see ~~through~~ by the dawn's early light
What so proudly we hail'd at the twilight's last gleaming,
Whose broad stripes & bright stars through the perilous fight
O'er the ramparts we watch'd, were so gallantly streaming?
And the rocket's red glare, the bomb bursting in air,
Gave proof through the night that our flag was still there
O say does that star spangled banner yet wave
O'er the land of the free & the home of the brave?

On the shore dimly seen through the mists of the deep,
Where the foe's haughty host in dread silence reposes,
What is that which the breeze, o'er the towering steep,
As it fitfully blows, half conceals, half discloses?
Now it catches the gleam of the morning's first beam,
In full glory reflected now shines in the stream,
'Tis the star-spangled banner — O long may it wave
O'er the land of the free & the home of the brave!

And where is that band who so vauntingly swore,
That the havoc of war & the battle's confusion
A home & a Country should leave us no more?
Their blood has wash'd out their foul footstep's pollution
No r
From the terror of flight or the gloom of the
And the star-spangled banner in triumph doth
O'er the land of the free & the home of the

Key's first copy of "Defence of Fort M'Henry"

Adding a Tune

Key wrote that the words for his poem could be sung to a **melody** called "To **Anacreon** in Heaven." People liked Key's new song, which became known as "The Star-Spangled Banner." The U.S. Congress named it the national anthem in 1931.

THE
STAR SPANGLED BANNER
A PARIOTIC SONG.
Baltimore. Printed and Sold at CARRS Music Store 36 Baltimore Street.
Air, Anacreon in Heaven.
Con Spirito
O! say can you see by the dawn's early light, What so
proudly we hail'd at the twilight's last gleaming, Whose broad stripes & bright stars thro' the
perilous fight, O'er the ramparts we watch'd, were so gallantly streaming. And the
Rockets' red glare, the Bombs bursting in air, Gave proof through the night that our
(Adapd & Arrd by T.C.)

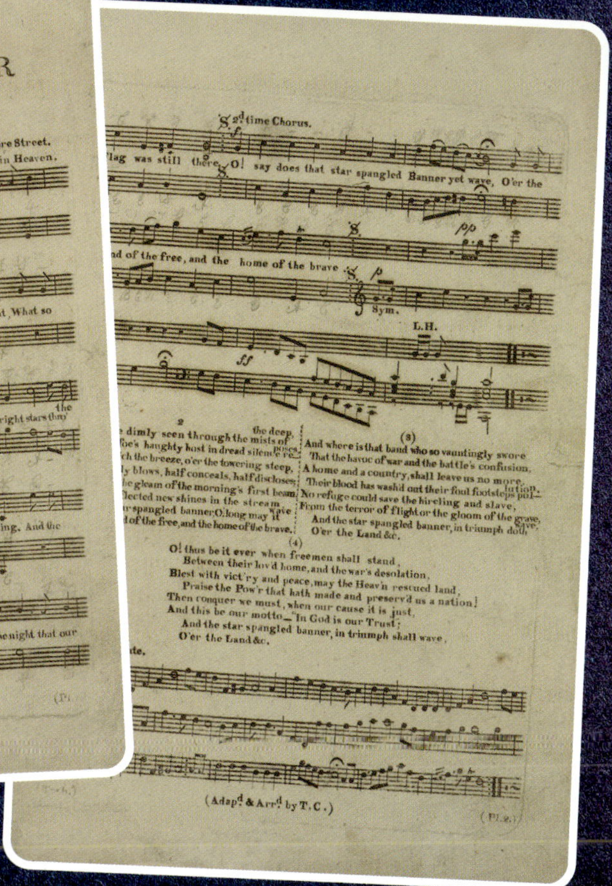
2d time Chorus.
flag was still there, O! say does that star spangled Banner yet wave, O'er the
land of the free, and the home of the brave.
Sym.
L.H.
O! thus be it ever when freemen shall stand,
Between their lov'd home, and the war's desolation,
Blest with vict'ry and peace, may the Heav'n rescued land,
Praise the Pow'r that hath made and preserv'd us a nation!
Then conquer we must, when our cause it is just,
And this be our motto_"In God is our Trust;"
And the star spangled banner, in triumph shall wave,
O'er the Land &c.
(Adapd & Arrd by T.C.)

The Anthem Today

Today, people sing "The Star-Spangled Banner" during special **ceremonies** and before sports events. There are four **verses**, but most sing only the first. Before the song is sung, it's a sign of respect for people to stand and remove their hats. Some put their right hand over their heart too.

History to Music

Next time you hear the anthem, listen to the words. Imagine what Francis Scott Key was seeing and thinking. The song means more now than what happened in battle. It's about the United States—"the land of the free and the home of the brave"—standing strong through hard times.

Know Your National Anthem: "The Star-Spangled Banner"

O say can you see, by the dawn's early light,

What so proudly we ***hail'd*** *at the twilight's last* ***gleaming****,*

Whose broad stripes and bright stars through the ***perilous*** *fight*

O'er the ***ramparts*** *we watch'd were so* ***gallantly*** *streaming?*

And the rocket's red ***glare****, the bombs bursting in air,*

Gave proof through the night that our flag was still there,

O say does that star-spangled banner yet wave

O'er the land of the free and the home of the brave?

hail'd = cheered

gleaming = shining

perilous = dangerous

ramparts = walls

gallantly = bravely

glare = shine

This is the first verse of "The Star-Spangled Banner."

GLOSSARY

Anacreon: An ancient Greek poet.

bombardment: An ongoing attack with guns or bombs.

celebrate: To honor with special activities.

ceremony: An event to honor or celebrate something.

melody: A tune, sometimes a part of a longer piece of music.

poem: A piece of writing in verse that sometimes tells a story.

prisoner: Someone who has been captured or locked up.

release: To let go or free.

represent: To stand for.

spangled: Having many decorations.

verse: One part of a song or poem.

FOR MORE INFORMATION

BOOKS

Earley, Christina. *National Anthem.* New York, NY: Crabtree Publishing Company, 2023.

Rustad, Martha E. H. *"The Star-Spangled Banner": America's National Anthem.* Minneapolis, MN: Lerner Publications, 2025.

WEBSITES

Francis Scott Key

kids.britannica.com/kids/article/Francis-Scott-Key/399517
Read more about this man, and find a link to learn about the War of 1812.

The Lyrics

amhistory.si.edu/starspangledbanner/the-lyrics.aspx
Read all of Key's words here.

Publisher's note to educators and parents: Our editors have carefully reviewed these websites to ensure that they are suitable for students. Many websites change frequently, however, and we cannot guarantee that a site's future contents will continue to meet our high standards of quality and educational value. Be advised that students should be closely supervised whenever they access the internet.

INDEX